MEASUREMENTS
Fun, Facts, and Activities

BY CAROLINE ARNOLD

Illustrated by Pam Johnson

An Easy-Read Geography Activity Book

Illustrated with drawings,
photographs,
and diagrams

A GROLIER COMPANY

Franklin Watts

New York London Toronto Sydney

1984

Photographs courtesy of Ewing Galloway: p. 7; Chicago Convention and Tourism Bureau: p. 10; Hobart Corporation: p. 12 (left and right); Brian Butler: p. 22 (left); Frank Sloan: p. 22 (right); F. Maraini/Monkmeyer Press Photo Service: p. 24.

R.L. 2.5 Spache Revised Formula

Library of Congress Cataloging in Publication

Arnold, Caroline.
Measurements : fun, facts, and activities.
(An Easy-read geography activity book)
Includes index.
Summary: Explains how things are measured, with directions for making counting sticks, a growth chart, a sand-clock timer, water-glass chimes, and other projects.
[1. Measurement.   2. Experiments.   3. Mathematical recreations]   I. Title.   II. Series.
QC39.A75 1984   530.8   84-7555
ISBN 0-531-04721-0

Contents

How Do We Measure?   5
Adding and Subtracting: Counting Sticks   7
Measuring Height: Make a Growth Chart   10
Measuring Weight: A Weight Guessing Game   12
Measuring Distance: How Far Is It?   14
Measuring Speed: How Fast Can You Go?   16
Measuring Time: A Sand-Clock Timer   18
Measuring Time: An Anytime Calendar   20
Measuring Liquids: Water-Glass Chimes   22
Measuring Temperature: How Cold Is It?   24
Measuring the Wind: A Butterfly Kite   26
Measuring Area: Big Cities and Small Towns   28
Words to Know   30
Index   32

How Do We Measure?

What kinds of things do we measure?
We measure height and weight to find out how
big things are.
We measure distances in and between our com-
munities.
We measure wind and temperature to find out
about the weather.
We use clocks to measure time.
You can have fun measuring things at home and
in your community.

Some people use the English system to measure
things.

This system began in England a long time ago.

Miles, inches, pounds, and quarts are some of the
units it uses.

Today in England people use the metric system
to measure things.

Meters, grams, and liters are some of the units in
the metric system.

Everything in the metric system is counted by tens.

People in the United States use both the English
and metric systems.

Many countries use just the metric system.

Look at some food packages at home or in a food
store.

Read the labels.

Do they give the measurements in English units,
metric units, or both?

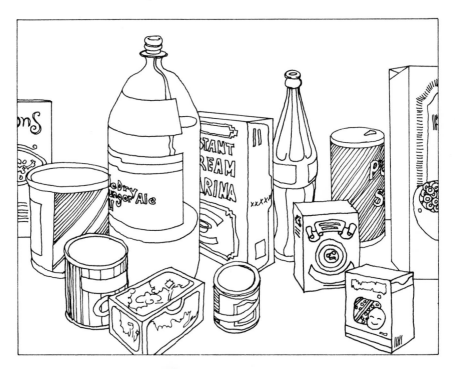

Adding and Subtracting: Counting Sticks

From the time we are small we learn to count
   things.
We count our fingers and toes.
We count how old we are.
We count the people in our family, city, state, and
   country.
Did you know that there are over 226 million
   people that live in the United States?
Sometimes we use adding machines and calcula-
   tors to help us count.
You can make some counting sticks to help you
   count.

You will need:
four wood skewers
a block of styrofoam
white glue
a marker
36 metal nuts (with holes big enough to fit over
the skewers)

First poke the skewers into the styrofoam.
Put them about 1 inch (2.5 cm) apart.

Glue them in place.

From right to left write the words "ones," "tens," "hundreds," and "thousands" in front of each skewer.

Use each skewer for one number place.

Use each metal nut for one number unit.

Here's how to make the number 6,204.

Put six nuts on the "thousands" stick.

Put two nuts on the "hundreds" stick.

Put no nuts on the "tens" stick.

Put four nuts on the "ones" stick.

Your counting sticks now show the number 6,204.

If you take away two nuts from the "ones" stick, what number do you have?

What do you have if you add two?

Measuring Height:
Make a Growth Chart

The tallest building in the world is in the city of
 Chicago.
How tall are you?
You can measure yourself with the English system
 in feet and inches.
Or you can use the metric system and measure
 yourself in meters.
Do you know how tall you were last year?
Do you know how much you have grown?
You can make a growth chart.
It will help you keep track of how fast you grow.

You will need:
a roll of white shelf paper
a yard- or meterstick or a measuring tape
a pencil
scissors
tape

Roll the paper out on the floor.
Cut off about 2 yards or 2 meters.
Use your measuring stick or tape to mark spaces
        1 inch or 1 decameter apart.
Label them.
Use the tape to hang your chart on the wall
        or on the back of a door.
Make sure the bottom is on the floor.
Stand next to it.
Have someone measure your height.
Mark it on the chart and write the date.
You may also want to measure the height of your
        friends and family.

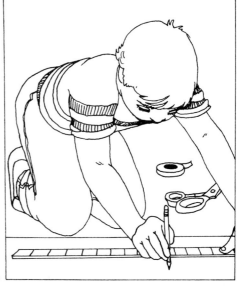

Measuring Weight:
A Weight Guessing Game

Do you know how much you weigh?
Your doctor uses a scale to weigh you when you
go for a checkup.
We use scales at the market to weigh fruits and
vegetables.
We use scales at the post office to weigh pack-
ages.
Some people have scales at home too.
In the English system we measure weight in
ounces, pounds, and tons.
The metric system uses grams, kilograms, and
metric tons to measure weight.
Here is a weight guessing game.
You can play it alone or with a friend.

You will need:
a postal or kitchen scale
a pencil
household objects such as cotton balls, a toothbrush,
    a toy car, a block, an apple, or a spoon
graph paper

First try to guess which of your objects weighs
    the most.
Then guess which weighs the least.
Then weigh the objects one at a time.
Write down the weights on a piece of paper.
Did you guess right?
You can make a bar graph to show how
    the weights compare.
Your bar graph might look something like this.

Apple								
Block								
Toothbrush								
Cotton								

Measuring Distance:
How Far Is It?

How far do you have to go to school? To go shopping? To visit your grandparents?

Places that are less than a mile (1.6 km) away are usually close enough to walk to.

But when places are farther away we often go in a bus or car.

You can find out how far you go by reading an
   odometer.
The odometer is on the dashboard of the car or
   bus.
It looks something like this.

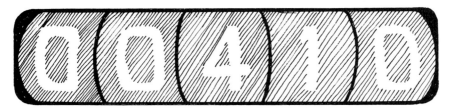

It shows how many miles or kilometers have been
   driven.
To measure how far you go on a trip you must look
   at the odometer when you start.
Write down the number.
For most trips you need to look at only the last
   three whole numbers.
Tenths of a mile are usually a different color.
Don't write down tenths of a mile.
At the end of your trip look at the odometer again.
Write down that number.
Subtract the first number from the second number.
Now you know how far you went.
The Brown family drove from Omaha to Kansas
   City.
When they started, the last three whole numbers
   of the odometer were 453.
When they got to Kansas City the last three num-
   bers were 654.
How far did they go?

Measuring Speed:
How Fast Can You Go?

You can find out how fast a car, bus, or truck goes
by looking at the speedometer.

The speedometer is on the dashboard.

When the car is stopped, the needle of the speedometer points to zero.

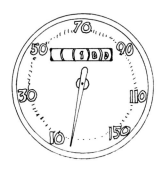

When the car is moving, the needle points to the
speed.

The speed is measured in the number of miles or
kilometers per hour.

If a car drives 30 miles (48 km) per hour for one
hour then it will go 30 miles.

Philadelphia and Lancaster are 60 miles (96 km)
apart.

How long would it take to drive from Philadelphia
to Lancaster at 30 miles per hour?

We measure speed by measuring time and distance.

You can have races with your friends.

You can use a stopwatch to find out how fast you
can go.

You will need:
a stopwatch
an open area

Mark a starting line.
Mark another line across the other end of the
   racing area.
Each racer must leave from the starting line,
   touch the other line, and come back.
Use the stopwatch to find out how long it takes.
You can have running races, hopping races,
   or skipping races.
The person who races in the shortest time wins.
You can practice to improve your speed.

Measuring Time:
A Sand-Clock Timer

We use clocks to measure time.
Some clocks have hands that go around.
Others don't have hands, but show the numbers.
    These are digital.
The first mechanical clock was invented around
    the year 1400 by a German.
A long time before that people sometimes made
    clocks with sand.
The sand flowed through a tiny hole from one con-
    tainer to another.
The clock measured how long it took for the con-
    tainer on the top to empty.
You can make a clock with sand too.

You will need:
a cone-shaped paper or plastic
    cup
a clear plastic cup
scissors
a pencil
a piece of heavy paper
a piece of wire screen
sand
a clock

Draw a circle on the paper.
Make it smaller than the top of the cone-shaped cup.
Cut it out.
Put the paper over the clear plastic cup.
Now cut just a little off the bottom of the
    cone-shaped cup.
You should have a small hole.
Put the cone-shaped cup in the hole of the paper.
Use the screen to sift out any rocks
    or lumps.
Then fill the cup with sand.
The sand will run out of the small hole into the other cup.
Look at the clock when you start.
How long did it take for the top cup to empty?
You can change the time by adding or taking away sand.

Measuring Time:
An Anytime Calendar

Each time the earth turns around is a new day.
We measure the days of the year with a calendar.
Here is a calendar you can make.
It will work for any month of any year.

You will need:
a board, about 12″ (30 cm) x
    6″ (15 cm)
nails
a hammer
a paper punch
a small tablet of paper
markers or crayons
a ruler and pencil

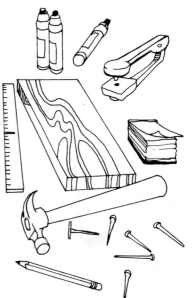

Use the ruler and pencil to
    draw a line across the top
    of the board.
On the line write the words
    "day," "month," and
    "date."

Under each word pound a
  nail partway in.
Now tear off seven sheets of
  paper.
On each sheet write a different day of the week.
Now punch a hole in the top
  of each sheet.
Put these sheets on the "day"
  nail.
Make sure the right day is on
  top.
Now make 12 month sheets.
Punch them and put them on
  the "month" nail.
Then number 31 sheets of paper from 1 to 31.
Put these on the "date" nail.
Each day you can change the
  day and the date sheets.
Each month you can change
  the month sheet.
With your anytime calendar
  you will always have the
  right day, month, and
  date.

Measuring Liquids:
Water-Glass Chimes

Did you know that over two-thirds of the world is
   covered with water?
Water is a liquid.
In the English system we measure liquids in cups,
   pints, quarts, and gallons.
In the metric system we measure liquids in liters
   and milliliters.
You can learn to measure liquids and make a set
   of water-glass chimes.

You will need:
water
eight drinking glasses
a measuring cup (2-cup or
     500-ml)
a metal spoon

Line up the empty glasses on a table.

Look at the side of the measuring cup.

Find the line marked ¼ cup or 62.5 ml.

Fill the cup with water to that line.

Make sure the cup is level when you measure.

Leave the first glass empty.

Pour the water into the second glass.

Now measure ⅓ cup or 83 ml
of water.

Pour it into the third glass.

Measure and pour ½ cup or 125 ml, ⅔ cup or 167 ml,
¾ cup or 187.5 ml, 1 cup
or 250 ml, and 1¼ cups
or 313 ml into the other
glasses.

Each glass should have a little more water in it
than the glass next to it.

Now use the spoon to gently tap each glass.

Does each glass make a different sound?

You can make up a tune to play on your water-glass
chimes.

Measuring Temperature:
How Cold Is It?

The Himalayas are the tallest mountains in the
world.
They are over 5 miles (8 km) high.
On top of the mountains the air is so cold that the
snow never melts.
In some parts of the world the air is so warm it
never snows at all.
We use a thermometer to measure temperature.
The liquid inside the glass of the thermometer
moves up when the temperature gets warm.
It goes down when the temperature is cold.
You can measure the temperature in Celsius or
Fahrenheit degrees.

Water freezes at 0 degrees Celsius and at 32 degrees Fahrenheit.

Water boils at 100 degrees Celsius and at 212 degrees Fahrenheit.

Can you read the temperature on this thermometer?

What is it in Celsius degrees?

What is it in Fahrenheit degrees?

How many ice cubes do you think you need to make a glass of hot water cold?

You can do an experiment to find out.

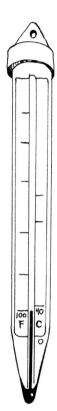

You will need:
a thermometer that can be put in water
     (not a fever thermometer)
a glass
hot water
ice cubes

Fill the glass half full of hot water.

Put in the thermometer. What is the temperature?

Now add the ice cubes one by one.

Can you see the temperature go down?

How many ice cubes did you need to make it 40 degrees Fahrenheit?
5 degrees Celsius?

Measuring the Wind:
A Butterfly Kite

We use the wind for energy and for transportation.
The wind helps us to cool off, to fly airplanes, and
to push windmills.
We need to measure both the speed and the direction of the wind.
At an airport you can sometimes see a wind sock.
It shows the wind direction.
You can make a kite to fly on windy days.

You will need:
a large grocery bag   scissors
a pencil   a stapler
masking tape   kite string
two crepe paper streamers,
    3 feet (.9m) long

First draw a butterfly shape on one large side
    of the bag.
Cut it out.
Put a strip of tape down the middle of the butterfly.
Carefully poke two small holes through the bag
    and the tape about
    6 inches (15 cm) apart.
Cut a piece of string about 18 inches (46 cm) long.
Tie it in a circle through the two holes.
Tie your kite string to the loop.
For the tail, staple the streamers to the bottom
    of the kite.
Now it is ready to fly.
If you wish you can draw designs on the kite too.

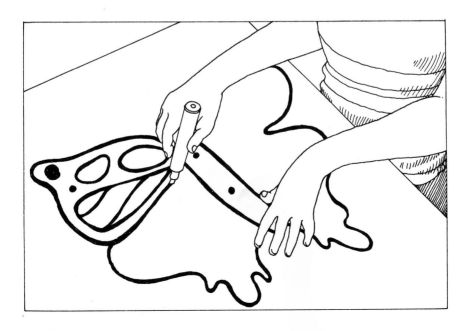

Measuring Area:
Big Cities and Small Towns

Some cities are very big.
In some places the city of Los Angeles is nearly
50 miles (80 km) across.
Most cities are much smaller.
The size of a city, state, or country is measured in
square miles or square kilometers.
A square mile is an area that is 1 mile wide and
1 mile long.
Do you know the area of your town or city?
You can make a map of an imaginary country on
graph paper.
Then you can measure the areas of the cities on
your map.

You will need:
graph paper
a pencil

Follow the lines of the squares to make several cities on your map.
Now you can count the squares to find out the
area of each city.
Which is the biggest?
If you wish you can add roads, train tracks, lakes,
or rivers to your imaginary map.

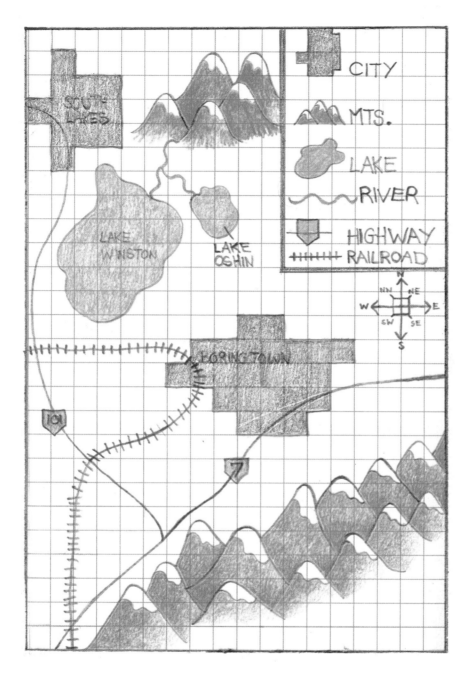

People measure all kinds of things every day.
Time, distance, weight, and temperature are some
    of the things we need to measure.
Measurements help us to find out about ourselves
    and the places we live.

Words to Know

Calculator. A machine that helps us count.

Calendar. A chart that lets us measure the days of the year.

Celsius. A way of measuring temperature. On the Celsius (or centigrade) scale, water freezes at 0°.

Decameter. Ten meters.

English System. Units of measurement that include miles, inches, pounds, and quarts.

Fahrenheit. A way of measuring temperature. On the Fahrenheit scale, water freezes at 32° above zero.

Metric System. A system of measuring that includes meters, grams, and liters. Everything is counted by tens.

Odometer. A measuring device on the dashboard of a car or bus. It shows how many miles or kilometers have been driven.

Scales. Instruments that tell us how much objects weigh.

Speedometer. A measuring device on the dashboard of a car, bus, or truck that tells how fast the vehicle is going.

Square Mile. An area that is one mile wide and one mile long.

Thermometer. An instrument for measuring temperature.

Index

Addition, 7, 9
Areas, measuring, 28

Bar graph, 13
Boiling point of water, 25

Calendars, 20–21
Celsius degrees, 24–25
Cities, measuring areas of, 28
Clocks, 18–19
Counting, 7–9
Counting sticks, 7–8

Decameters, 11
Decimal system, 9
  in metric system, 6
Degrees of temperature, 24–25
Digital clocks, 18
Distance, measuring, 14

English system of measurement,
  6

Fahrenheit degrees, 24–25
Freezing point of water, 15

Growth chart, 10–11

Height, measuring, 10–11

International Date Line, 20

Kilometers, 6, 14
Kite, making a, 26–27

Labels on food packages, 6
Liquids, measuring, 22–23

Liters, 22

Maps, 28
Meters, 6, 10
Metric system, 6
  area measurement in, 28
  distance in, 14
  height in, 10–11
  liquid measurement in, 22–23
  speed in, 16
  weight in, 6, 12
Miles traveled, 15
Mountains, 24

Odometer, 15

Place value, 9

Sand-clock timer, 18–19
Scales, 12–13
Speed, measuring, 16–17
Speedometer, 16
Square kilometers, 28
Square miles, 28
Stopwatch, 16–17
Subtraction, 9, 15

Temperature, measuring, 24–25
Thermometers, 24–25
Time, measuring, 18–21
Towns, measuring areas of, 28

Water, 22–23
Water-glass chimes, 22–23
Weight, measuring, 12
Wind direction, 26
Wind, measuring, 26–27